FORTUNE TELLERS
Club

THE
BURNING
PENDULUM

D0391415

FORTUNE TELLERS Club

THE
BURNING
PENDULUM

DOTTI ENDERLE

Llewellyn Publications
St. Paul, Minnesota

FIRST EDITION
First printing, 2005

Book design and editing by Kimberly Nightingale
Cover design by Kevin R. Brown
Cover illustration and interior illustrations © 2005 by Matthew Archambault
Handwritten notes by Zora Fosse
Tarot card images are from the International Icon Tarot by Robin Ator, and are used with permission

Library of Congress Cataloging-in-Publication Data
(Pending)

ISBN: 0-7387-0435-0

Llewellyn Publications
A Division of Llewellyn Worldwide, Ltd.
P.O. Box 64383, Dept. 0-7387-0435-0
St. Paul, MN 55164-0383, U.S.A.
www.llewellyn.com

Printed in the United States of America

Other Books by Dotti Enderle

The Lost Girl
Playing with Fire
The Magic Shades
Secrets of Lost Arrow
Hand of Fate
Mirror, Mirror . . .

A special thanks to Robin Ator
for saving the day.

—D

Contents

CHAPTER 1 The Assignment . . . 1

CHAPTER 2 Grave Dangers . . . 9

CHAPTER 3 The Wrath of Mom . . . 19

CHAPTER 4 Threatened . . . 33

CHAPTER 5 Library Refuge . . . 43

CHAPTER 6 Nowhere to Hide . . . 55

CHAPTER 7 Message Received . . . 65

CHAPTER 8 Marble Magic . . . 75

CHAPTER 9 Negotiating . . . 85

CHAPTER 10 The Top Ten . . . 93

CHAPTER 11 Extra! Extra! . . . 101

CHAPTER 12 The Verdict . . . 109

CHAPTER 13 Cockeyed Confessions . . . 121

CHAPTER 1

The Assignment

Juniper waited, nervously flicking the pages of the paperback book she held. When that didn't calm her, she fidgeted with the circular pendulum that had come with it. She wanted to ease her jitters but they kept building, stronger and stronger, until she thought she might spontaneously combust. She closed her eyes, thinking of her nerves as computer data, even trying to envision a delete button, but that didn't work. Her anxiety simply multiplied like email spam.

Regan Wells was finishing her oral book report, and Juniper was next. "So that's why it's important that I donate *Buffalo Soldiers* to our new school library—as a tribute to my great-great-great-grandfather. He served as a buffalo soldier in the Civil War and I donate this book in his name."

Mrs. Blum's clapping aroused the drowsy class, and a few kids joined in the applause. "Well done, Regan." She consulted a list on her desk, scanning it through her reading glasses. "Juniper. You're next."

Juniper clamored to the front, holding the book and pendulum like a wad of tissues. She wished she could dance the report instead of speak it. She never got nervous during her dance recitals. Slowly, she held up the book for the class to see. Her mouth was completely dry, like she'd been chewing on her pillow.

"When we were asked to donate our favorite book for the new library, I sort of had a problem picking just one. See, my favorite books are in a series." The classroom snickering made her pause.

That's when she noticed the book was upside down. Flipping it around, she continued. "This is *Grave Dangers,* the third book in the Psychic Circle series. The third one is really the best of the series, I think."

She looked around at the moon-faced kids staring up at her. Some were nodding, obviously familiar with the Psychic Circle. Others had eyes glazed over from hearing too many oral reports in one hour. They'd obviously shut out all new incoming information for the day.

"The Psychic Circle is a group of teenagers who each have different psychic abilities. Using E.S.P. and other forms of mind-reading, they solve mysteries. In *Grave Dangers,* they solve the mystery of who's really buried in a creepy old grave marked 'Glover Handlestein.'" More nods from the kids who were actually listening.

"They also have lots of supernatural stuff. Like in this book, they see zombies coming up from the family cemetery. It's so cool. I really get caught up in this series. I think that J. D. Devers is the best author ever."

"You know there is no J. D. Devers," Nicole Hoffman spouted. "That's just a made-up name. They hire different writers to write those books."

"That's called 'ghost writing,'" Mrs. Blum added.

"I knew that," Juniper said, clutching the book with white knuckles. But she hadn't really known. Her heart sank like a yo-yo. She'd always imagined J. D. Devers as an old-looking Mark Twain fellow, writing on an ancient typewriter and surrounded by candles, E.S.P. cards, and pictures of astrological symbols covered in milky cobwebs. And it was especially painful to learn the truth from one of the Snotty Twins.

"Anyway, here's the best part." She dangled the pendulum in front of her. It was nothing more than a jade-colored plastic ring attached to a length of waxed purple string, but its presence caused the kids to sit up at their desks. The droopy fog had cleared, giving the air a perky feel. Juniper had them.

"Each book comes with a special device that lets you play along and guess the outcome.

Grave Dangers comes with a pendulum." She opened the book and thumbed through to a particular page. "Here's how it works. At the end of each chapter there is a set of clues. In some of the books, the clues are written. In this one, there are pictures. You hold the pendulum over the page and concentrate."

She closed her eyes, letting the pendulum hang limp over the page of clues. She didn't concentrate because she already knew the answer. It would be easy. She'd read this particular book three times. But for some reason, her arm tingled, just as it did when she was doing real psychic work. She cleared her mind, focusing on the pendulum. In just a matter of seconds it started to swing, slightly at first, then in large sweeping motions. A few *Oooooooos* rose up from the class.

"The pendulum will swing toward a clue," Juniper continued. "That's how you try to solve the mystery along with the Psychic Circle." But it didn't swing toward the clue. Instead it heated up, the string circling wide and counterclockwise. *Odd.* Was the pendulum trying to tell her something?

She stopped the swinging pendulum and laid it down on the book. *What was that all about?* She blocked the confusion and continued her report. "I'm pretty good at it, myself. I've never missed yet on solving a case before the end of the book." She decided not to tell them about the tingling sensation she has when she works with different forms of divination. Or that it had happened right then! Most of the kids already knew it was her passion anyway, and a few even knew about the Fortune Tellers Club.

"So . . . I'm going to donate *Grave Dangers,* and three other Psychic Circle books, to Mrs. Thompson for the new library."

Juniper quickly scooted back to her desk. She was so glad the book report was over and that hers was the last one for today. Her throat felt like the Sahara, and she desperately needed a drink of water—make that a gallon.

"Can I see that?"

Juniper turned in her desk and handed the book to Caitlin Greeley, sitting kitty-corner across the aisle. She watched Caitlin skim the book with interest, pausing to read a sentence or two. "Thanks," she told Juniper, handing it back.

"I'd loan it to you, but it's for the library," Juniper said.

"That's okay."

The bell rang, causing the usual hurried scuffling and loud voices. Juniper gathered her things for the next class. She was sure she'd done well with the report, but still, something didn't seem right. She clutched the pendulum, then instantly loosened her grip. Still hot . . . too hot. Why doesn't it melt the plastic? She glanced out the window on her way to the door. Sunny and beautiful out. *Hmmm* . . . why did she feel like a storm was brewing? Something was definitely up. She could smell it in the air.

CHAPTER 2

Grave Dangers

"Aren't you going to say anything?" Anne asked.

Juniper leaned against the old magnolia tree in the school yard, wishing the bell would ring before Anne and Gena got into a tiff.

Gena still had a look of mild shock on her face. "Would you repeat that?" she asked. "I thought I heard you say that you like Kyle Morgan."

Anne slumped. "Come on, guys, you have to admit—he's gotten really cute."

9

"Kyle Morgan?" Gena asked, blinking and rattling her head. "As in a.k.a. Booger Boy?"

Anne looked about ready to slug Gena with her backpack. "Oh, come on. That was in second grade!"

"And third, fourth, fifth . . . give me a break, Anne."

Juniper stepped in. "You really think he's cute, huh? I still can't get that booger-eating image out of my head."

"Have you seen him lately?" Anne asked.

"Yeah, he's let his hair grow out a little and combs it differently."

"I think he should comb it over his nose," Gena said. "That way we wouldn't have to see him pick his lunch."

"Fine," Anne said, turning her nose up slightly. "You won't have to see anyway. I'm sitting with him during lunch. You guys can sit across the room."

"Except that we have assigned tables," Gena smirked. "So you and Booger Boy sit at one end and we'll sit at another."

"I don't think we're being fair," Juniper said. She didn't want to sit away from Anne because of some boy—especially Kyle Morgan, whose reputation was built solely on immature snacking habits.

The bell rang before anything was solved. The girls headed toward the side doors of the school.

★　★　★

Juniper hated starting her day with mixed feelings. She woke up in a good mood, thinking about her dance solo for the school talent show next week, the extra bonus points she scored in science yesterday, and the missed classes tomorrow afternoon for the new library dedication ceremony. *Things were great. Right?* So why did she have a feeling they weren't?

There were only seven minutes left in first period when Juniper heard the beep of the intercom. She automatically knew the first storm clouds had rolled in.

"Would you send Juniper Lynch to the office, please?"

The class shuffled in their seats, watching her. She silently loaded her book and papers into her backpack and walked out. She didn't hurry, but she didn't slack either. *How bad could it be?* She'd never been in any real trouble in her life—especially in school.

The principal's office smelled of lilac—or the dregs of an overpowering lilac perfume. Juniper preferred the stiff, leathery smell she had encountered the few times she'd been in here. Maybe the student who sat here before was called in from gym class and did a fast stink-cover job with a bottle of cologne.

Mr. Chapman hurried in and sat down behind his desk. Juniper's heart jumped when she saw he was holding *Grave Dangers*.

"Juniper, I'm sorry to pull you out of class like this, but I just had a parent here who was quite upset."

Juniper sniffed the lilac air—definitely not a dad.

"She was upset about the book report you presented in English class yesterday."

"What did I do wrong?" Juniper asked, her voice cracking from nerves. She could see that Mr. Chapman was choosing his words carefully.

"It's not so much about right and wrong as it is about tastes . . . uh . . . and beliefs. This book you chose to do your report on, well, it contains some supernatural content."

Juniper relaxed. "So I'm not the only one in trouble." She thought about Jason Griggs doing his report on the third Harry Potter book. *Who else reported on supernatural books yesterday?* Her mind whirled to remember.

"You're not exactly in trouble, but your demonstration involved divination. Some people find that unsuitable, as does the school. Now, I managed to calm this parent down with a simple agreement: you'd pick a more appropriate book for the school library."

"But the teacher asked us to donate our favorite books," Juniper said, confused.

Mr. Chapman nodded. "I understand, but Juniper, let's not make a big deal over this, okay? I mean, it's just a flimsy paperback anyway." He bent back the spine and pages to demonstrate his point.

"I was going to donate more than one," Juniper offered, feeling strange about this whole thing.

Mr. Chapman rose and came around. Sitting down on the corner of his desk, he folded his hands and smiled. "You are one of our top students. Excellent grades, involved in school activities, and you show good citizenship."

She slumped. Nothing was worse than being talked down to by school authorities.

"So, as a favor to me and yourself, choose another book."

Juniper nodded and rose. She forced a slight smile at Mr. Chapman and walked toward his office door. "Oh yeah—uh—sir? Can I have my book back?"

"It'll be here for you after school."

★ ★ ★

At lunch, Juniper didn't care that Kyle Morgan was sitting next to Anne at their usual lunch table. She scooted onto the bench across from them. Gena slid in next to her.

"I was called to the principal's office this morning," Juniper blurted.

Gena, Anne, and Kyle all stopped and stared. They looked at her like she'd sprouted horns and two extra eyes. She told the whole story while they unpacked their sandwiches, chips, and assorted sweets.

"That's stupid," Gena said, smooshing her peanut butter sandwich into a pancake-like treat. The imprint of her palm stayed on the bread.

"Yeah, it is," Juniper agreed, as she watched Gena roll the sandwich up and take a big bite. "But I don't want to make anyone mad."

"I think Psychic Circle is stupid," Kyle said, ripping the foil lid off his pudding.

Juniper sure didn't need his opinion. "It's not as stupid as eating your dessert first."

"At least it didn't come out of his schnozzle," Gena said.

Anne and Kyle both shot her a look with flame-thrower eyes.

"I just don't feel right about this," Juniper continued. "How come Jason can donate a Harry Potter book, but I can't donate mine?"

"Did you ask Mr. Chapman about that?" Anne asked.

"No, I was too chicken. Anyway, it's not fair."

Kyle dipped his finger in his pudding and brought up a big chocolate heap. "This is what I think of Psychic Circle." He smeared a giant brown streak across his tray.

"Have you ever read a Psychic Circle book?" Juniper asked.

"Heck, no! I'm not that dumb."

"Then how can you have an opinion about books you haven't read?"

Kyle licked the chocolate off his finger. "Get real. It's a group of teenagers who go around messing with *astrology* and *magic* and other fake junk. The whole idea is lame."

Juniper's blood grew warmer and she could feel her face flush. Anne squirmed a bit, not looking up. Before Juniper could speak, Gena jumped in.

"The whole idea of you being Anne's boyfriend is lame! It's obvious you don't have anything in common, other than she likes your new hairstyle. So just keep your opinions to yourself from now on, okay Booger Boy?"

Kyle aimed his juice box and squeezed, sending a stream of orange-pineapple liquid on Gena's face.

"Kyle!" Anne warned.

Gena snatched a stack of sour cream and onion potato chips and smashed them on top of Kyle's ketchup sandwich. "And here," she said, flinging a pickle chip that had fallen from Juniper's tuna, "nice and juicy and green."

Juniper shut out their babyish behavior, feeling betrayed that Anne sat quietly, observing the fiasco but not defending the Fortune Tellers Club. Kyle Morgan may not sample from the nose factory anymore, but he didn't have a right to smear her favorite series like he'd smeared the pudding. This day was getting worse by the minute—and it was only half over.

CHAPTER 3

The Wrath of Mom

"What?" Juniper's mom stared at her as though she hadn't actually heard what Juniper had said. Mom took a deep breath, then clinched her fists. "What!"

Juniper just shrugged. She was afraid if she said anything else it'd be adding fuel to the fire.

"Juniper, you cannot be serious!" Mom leaned against the kitchen sink, shaking her head. She had been basting a steak in Italian dressing when Juniper related the story. Joy Lynch hated things bland, particularly food. It was one of the things Juniper loved best about her.

Juniper backed up a few steps as her mom grabbed the steak and flipped it in the pan of dressing. She actually slapped it back into the oil like she was swatting a fly. "Do you know what you're telling me? Do you know what that is?"

Whether she did or not, Juniper kept quiet. She was sure Mom was about to step up on her soapbox and give her the full details.

"That's book banning, Juniper! Book banning!" She turned back to the sink and grabbed a dish rag. "In this day and age! Outrageous."

Juniper thought she might use the rag to wipe up the splattered dressing from the angry slap; but instead, Mom wrung it around and around—hopefully, to control her temper.

"You will take that book back to school tomorrow. You'll give it to Mrs. Thompson for the library. Understood?"

"But I promised Mr. Chapman . . . "

Mom glared her way. "Take the book back tomorrow."

Juniper tried to swallow, but the spit stuck in her throat. "I'll get in trouble."

Mom closed her eyes and let out a ragged breath. "You won't get in trouble. I won't let that happen."

Before she could protest again, Mom grabbed the phone and started punching buttons. *Fine.* Juniper wanted to hide out in her room for a while anyway.

She passed Jonathan, sitting in front of his favorite afternoon TV shows—though slumping seemed more like it. His leg was hanging over the arm of the chair, and his dirty sneaker was half on and half off, dangling on his toes. Juniper tried to sneak by.

"What'd you do to make Mom mad?"

Too late. "I didn't do anything."

"I heard her yelling."

"The whole town heard her yelling. You know how she gets." There were times when Juniper wished she didn't know.

Jonathan peeked up over the chair arm. "You must have done something real bad."

"I did," Juniper confessed. "I told her you snuck half a package of Oreos in here and wolfed 'em down right before dinner."

Jonathan shot straight up, looking like a ghost. "Uh-uh. How'd you know?"

Juniper grinned. "I'm psychic." She sauntered off to her room, not daring to tell the little twerp that only Oreos could cause his teeth to be caked in that awful black goo.

Since Mom was tying up the phone, Juniper sent Anne and Gena an email.

Subject: F TC Meeting

URGENT!
We need to meet tonight. Please say you both can make it.

J.

She reached in her backpack, tugging out her books and folders for homework. *Grave Dangers* fell out onto the floor, spread open, facedown. Juniper picked it up and looked at the open page. It was one that contained a list of clues. Five small pictures forming an X: a book, a violin, an ivy trellis, a dog, and a mailbox. Juniper remembered that the clue needed in this story was the violin. But somehow she felt the fall was no accident. The book obviously opened to this page to tell her something. She picked up the pendulum and held it over the clues. Not hot this time, but she did detect a buzz trembling through it. The string jiggled a little, then began to swing. Juniper felt the tingling in her hand. She closed her eyes and emptied her mind of everything—something she achieved by concentrating on the darkness of her eyelids. The pendulum swung harder, the tingling grew stronger, and she couldn't tell where her fingers ended and the string began. It was a part of her. She took a deep breath, then opened her eyes. The jade circle stopped swinging. It stood stiff and tilted kitty-corner in midair . . . pointing toward the dog.

Startled, she grabbed the pendulum with her left hand. It had warmed up again. She'd fully expected it to swing slightly, indicating the book.

The warmth seemed comforting for some reason. She decided to slip the pendulum over her head and wear it like a necklace. It felt right there. Then she closed the book and went on with her homework.

★ ★ ★

"Wow, your mom is steamed," Anne said, sprawled out on the floor with her knees up. "She called my mom and got her all in a huff."

"You think that's bad, you should have seen her at dinner. And Dad wasn't exactly thrilled about it either." Juniper leaned against the foot of her bed, feeling limp and drained.

"What are you going to do?" Gena asked.

"Mom told me to take the book straight to Mrs. Thompson at the library, but I'd already told Mr. Chapman that I'd bring a different book. ."

"Ooooooh," Gena said. "This is starting to smell like week-old pork."

"Yeah. She and some other moms are going to be at the dedication ceremony tomorrow. Mom promised not to make a big stink, but I can smell that week-old pork already."

Anne sat up and tugged on the hem of her capris. "What are you going to do? Anything?"

"Heck, I don't know. That's why I wanted you guys over. I think we can come up with some answers using this." She held up the pendulum without removing it from around her neck.

"Not specific enough," Anne said. "Let's spread the tarot instead, and see what it says."

Juniper dug out the tarot cards.

"Let me," Anne said, reaching over and taking them. "You should distance yourself a little for a better reading. After all, it is about you."

"Actually, it's about the book," Gena said. "Maybe you should've just kept your mouth shut and brought in another one. I learned years ago not to tell my dad about what happens at school."

Anne stopped shuffling. "That's because most of it will get you grounded! This is different."

Gena grinned. "You're right. Spread the cards."

Anne withdrew the first card and placed it in front of her. The Hierophant.

"Who's that dude with a turkey on his head?" Gena asked.

"That's not a turkey," Juniper said. "I think this has something to do with a girl."

Gena snickered. "Because she's wearing a tiara?"

"Forget the head gear," Anne said. "What's that he's holding? It looks like some kind of antenna."

Juniper looked closer. "See the keys?"

Anne squinted. "What are you thinking?"

"I'm not sure," Juniper said. "The keys tell me that something is locked away, but the antenna reminds me of sound waves or radar."

"Like a TV or radio broadcast?" Gena asked.

Juniper shrugged. "I guess. You think the Snotty Twins are involved?"

"What?" Anne looked puzzled.

"Yeah," Gena said. "The little bald guys, the keys—things are doubled."

"Please don't let it be anything to do with Beth and Nicole," Juniper pleaded. "Turn up the next card."

Anne did. The Seven of Cups. "Hmmm . . . choices?"

"Obvious choices," Juniper said, looking at the Seven of Cups overflowing with different objects, good and bad.

Gena giggled. "Who's under the sheet?"

"I don't know," Anne said, "But look at the person in front. Suppose that guy didn't represent the person being read? What if the guy in the sheet did?"

"Can you say that in English?" Gena teased.

"She's making sense." Juniper suddenly looked at the card differently. "What if that person with the sheet or shroud on was me? I'm surrounded by all my victories and defeats. And see, the person in front is the one in control."

"But you are in control of your victories and defeats," Anne said.

"Am I? What about fate? Who controls that?"

Gena sat up on her knees. "Whoa . . . you guys are getting way too heavy for me. I think it's simply about choice, like we said before. Period."

Anne turned up another card. The Devil.

"This one's easy enough to interpret," Gena said. "You're going to have a devil of a time ahead."

Juniper gave her a look. "Ha, ha. If only it were that easy."

"Ew, look! He's set that guy's tail on fire." Anne pointed to the chained man in the picture.

"Why do these people have tails anyway?" Gena asked.

THE DEVIL.

Juniper continued to stare at the card. The pendulum heated up again, warming her as well. She stared hard at the tarot card, not wanting to miss a tiny detail. "He kinda has his hand up same as The Hierophant."

"So what do you think it's telling you?" Anne asked.

Juniper looked up at Anne, then Gena. "Whoever The Hierophant represents is a fake. It's all about deception."

Gena snorted. "Oink, oink. This pork is starting to smell worse than a week old."

Juniper shivered. "It's rotten, all right."

CHAPTER 4

Threatened

Students, teachers, and parents packed the auditorium. The buzz of voices lifted higher and higher as more came in and took a seat. Juniper spotted her mom in the front row. *Oh no.* She must have gotten here at least forty-five minutes early to get *that* close. She sat with a string of her friends who also had students at Avery Middle School. Anne's mom was among them. Anne was perched across the room, sitting with Kyle Morgan.

Juniper closed her eyes, inhaling deeply. She could smell the dusty fabric of the faded green curtains, closed tight and still. The *click click* of shoes crossed the stage and she opened her eyes. There stood Mr. Chapman behind a podium, with Mrs. Thompson sitting behind him.

"Welcome, students, parents, friends, and family. I am Dave Chapman, principal here at Avery. It's so nice to have this overwhelming turnout—but not surprising. We've learned in the last few months that no community anywhere is greater than ours. You each stepped forward when we needed you most, donating your money, time, and books so that Avery can again have a superior school library."

The audience broke into applause. Gena leaned forward near Juniper's ear. "Our library was superior?"

Juniper turned toward her. "Yeah. It even had books in it. You should have gone in occasionally."

Gena giggled. "I'm allergic to research."

Mr. Chapman carried on with details about the rebuilding process, then he smiled. "I think our gratitude could be expressed more richly by our librarian, Mrs. Thompson."

Mrs. Thompson stood, gathering her notes. Juniper had never seen her so dressed up. Her light blue suit reminded Juniper of the bluebonnets blooming along the highway in the spring. Mrs. Thompson smoothed back her golden hair and smiled.

"Let me say right off, you have built a library I could live in!"

The parents laughed and clapped. Gena leaned in again. "I thought she *did* live there."

Juniper snickered, and so did two girls next to them who overheard.

Mrs. Thompson continued—smiling and thanking as she shuffled her notes and occasionally shifted from leg to leg.

She's pretty good at this, Juniper thought. *She should have been the speech teacher.*

She ended by inviting everyone to visit the library this week, and reminding the parents that she could always use volunteers to help shelve the books. During the applause, a woman stood up in the third row. She held up her hand like a student wanting permission to speak. The room grew quiet.

"Mrs. Thompson," the woman said, her voice projecting clearly. "I just wanted to say how much we appreciate you, and the fine job you've done here at Avery. And we all trust that you'll use your good judgment to provide our children with wholesome, quality books they can cherish."

More applause. Juniper noticed her mom wasn't clapping.

"Thank you, Mrs. Greeley," Mrs. Thompson said. "I do my best."

Joy Lynch stood. She was holding a bag from the local bookstore.

Oh please, Mom. Don't do it!

"I'd like to add my gratitude too," Joy Lynch said. "And not only that, as a donation I've brought you the entire collection of my daughter's favorite series."

Juniper glanced at Mr. Chapman, who had now gone a milky shade of white. Mrs. Thompson continued to smile.

"I hope that's not the appalling series that caused such a ruckus the other day at school," Mrs. Greeley said, her frosted hair springing as she tossed her head side to side.

"I spoke with the teacher," Juniper's mom said. "There wasn't any ruckus."

"She brought witchcraft into the school!"

"She brought her favorite book into the school!"

Juniper slumped further and further down into her chair. The auditorium was as silent as a tomb, except for the shouts of her mom and Mrs. Greeley. And the tension was so thick she could have stuck candles in it and sang "Happy Birthday."

"Ladies," Mr. Chapman interrupted, scrambling to the microphone. "Let's continue this in my office."

The students moaned in unison as the teachers rose to line them up. There was still thirty minutes left before school let out for the day. Juniper tried to blend in with her class, but her mom spotted her in the crowd and motioned her over.

Why me, Lord? Juniper trudged against the one-way traffic of kids.

"I'd like you to sit with me in the office, okay?" Mom said, smoothing Juniper's hair off her shoulder.

"Do I have to?"

Mom didn't answer. She gave Juniper a look that showed she had no choice.

Joy Lynch said goodbye to the moms she'd been sitting with. They all gave her a thumbs up or a quick "good luck." Juniper had a feeling her mom didn't need any luck. She was a woman with a cause, and she wouldn't stop until it was mission accomplished.

Juniper shuffled up the aisle with her mom's hand on her shoulder. She was starting to feel a little queasy over this whole thing. *Why didn't I just keep my big mouth shut and get a different book?*

As they turned into Mr. Chapman's office, Juniper could see Mrs. Greeley already there, tapping her long pink nails on the arm of her chair. A tiny little face popped out of the tote bag next to her. Mrs. Greeley reached over and petted a tiny poodle.

As they walked by, Juniper could smell lilac again, but she realized it wasn't Mrs. Greeley's cologne after all. It came from the little dog, all powdered and fluffed with a teensy red bow on his head.

Mr. Chapman shifted some folders out of the way and leaned in on his desk. "Ladies, I think we'll be able to solve this in a reasonable fashion."

"I feel I'm being quite reasonable by insisting that those trashy, wicked books are not allowed in our library," Mrs. Greeley said.

Joy Lynch leaned in too. Juniper could read the determination in her face. "Mrs. Greeley, are you familiar with the First Amendment?"

"Don't patronize me, Mrs. Lynch. This has nothing to do with the First Amendment."

"This has everything to do with it!" her mother shouted.

"Ladies," Mr. Chapman interrupted. "Let's stay civil about this."

"Mrs. Lynch, you're lucky that I brought this issue to our school principal, and not the school board itself." Mrs. Greeley smirked, never taking her eyes off Juniper's mom.

"Mrs. Greeley, I don't care what you say or do. What you're proposing here is book banning. It's wrong and you know it."

Mrs. Greeley snapped like a spring. "You think I've done something wrong? My dear, it was your daughter who contaminated the class with all that witchcraft. There is no place in this school for voodoo."

"It's not witchcraft," Juniper said, suddenly relieved that she'd left the pendulum at home. "It's divination."

"It's wicked!" Mrs. Greeley barked. "Mr. Chapman," she said, turning her attention to him. "What are you going to do?"

Mr. Chapman removed his glasses and rubbed his eyes with his fingers. "I'm considering it. There must be a way to solve this peaceably."

Juniper's mom looked toward the door, then back to Mr. Chapman. "Why isn't Mrs. Thompson here? Doesn't this concern her too?"

"Stay calm, Mrs. Lynch," he said, sliding his glasses back on. "Let's try not to involve too many people."

"But she's the librarian!"

Juniper knew her mom was right. Mrs. Thompson should have the final say on what was put into the library.

"Mrs. Lynch, I'm going to ask that you give me some time to think this through," Mr. Chapman said. "School is letting out for the day. Let's take some time to cool off, and then we'll decide the best course for this."

Mrs. Greeley rose, snatching up her purse, then cradling her lilac-scented pooch. "Come, Sweetums, let's get away from this crazy place."

She pushed past Juniper and her mom, stomping toward the exit. "Oh yes, Mr. Chapman," she said, turning back. "I will not be intimidated, nor will I have my daughter subjected to evil. Your lack of a decision this afternoon tells me that you're clearly not doing your job. You can count on this going to the school board. And not only will I keep that garbage out of this library, I'll see to it that little Miss Juniper here is suspended for what's she's done."

Juniper felt her face grow hot and panicky. She kept her hand clamped on Mom's shoulder to keep herself from jumping up and going at it with Mrs. Greeley.

"I'll see you at the school board meeting," Joy Lynch said calmly.

Juniper couldn't wait to get out of there. She wanted to be home, watching TV or surfing the Internet. Even homework sounded better than all this. Mr. Chapman nodded as they left, and Juniper couldn't help but wonder what he'd decide to do. Would he really suspend his star pupil?

CHAPTER 5

Library Refuge

"Where were you guys last night?" Juniper asked as she approached Anne and Gena. They were waiting for her in their usual spot—the magnolia tree at the back of the school yard.

"I went to the hospital," Gena said.

"What?" Gena's statement startled Juniper. Anne looked surprised too.

Gena rolled her eyes. "Not as a patient. I went with Rachael and Dad to pick up Rachael's wallet.

She left it by the Coke machine in the nurse's lounge."

"Well, why didn't you just say so?" Juniper said. "I thought you were going to say you'd had a seizure or something."

"I kinda did," Gena joked. "I tried to squirm my way out of going, and when Dad said no, I had a seizure."

"That's a tantrum, not a seizure," Anne said.

Gena smiled. "I'm too old for tantrums. It was definitely a seizure."

"More like a fit, I bet," Juniper corrected. She looked at Anne. "And where were you?"

Anne shrugged. "I was home . . . sitting out in the front yard with a friend."

"Booger Boy!" Gena said. "Anne, will you please come to your senses?"

Anne shot Gena a few eye daggers. "I'm not going to talk about it, okay?"

Juniper didn't want to hear about it anyway. She had bigger problems than Anne's taste in boyfriends. "Doesn't anyone want to know what happened after the dedication?"

They both perked up, heads popping to attention. "I heard your mom threatened Mrs. Greeley," Anne said.

Juniper jerked in surprise. "That's not true! Where did you hear that?" Juniper was stunned that gossip had spread so soon. Especially since they hadn't talked to a soul about what happened in Mr. Chapman's office.

"I heard it from Kyle," Anne answered.

Gena snickered. "Of course. The guy who thinks fortune telling is lame. He's a real expert."

"What did he say?" Juniper asked, ignoring Gena.

"He said that your mom told Mrs. Greeley that if she didn't back down, she would put a major hex on her."

Juniper's heart sank like a stone. "And where did he get this information?"

"He heard it from Caitlin Greeley."

"She wasn't even there!" Juniper argued. "How would she know?"

"Maybe that little rat dog told her," Gena said. "He looks like a real snitch."

Anne giggled, but Juniper was close to having a seizure herself. How dare they spread lies about her mom.

Anne sighed, wiping the smile off her face. "Get real, Juniper. Don't you think Caitlin got that info from her mother?"

"Did you tell Kyle it was a lie?"

"I told him I didn't believe it. I know your mom would never say a thing like that. She doesn't even do hexes, does she?"

"No," Juniper said, "but if anyone makes up any more lies about her, I'll do my own hexing."

"The wrath of Juniper," Gena said, making a power fist.

"Mrs. Greeley is the one who did the threatening," Juniper continued. "She's saying she'll have me suspended."

Now it was Gena and Anne's turn for surprise. They looked like Juniper had told them there would be no Christmas this year. "She can't do that, can she?" Anne asked.

Juniper shrugged. "You tell me. She's reporting my behavior to the school board."

The bell rang and the girls shuffled to pick up their backpacks. "I bet your mom is really ticked now," Gena said as they walked to the side doors.

Juniper nodded. "I feel like I've started World War III."

★   ★   ★

Everyone stared at Juniper as they filed into the classroom. Some with sour looks, some with sneers, some with awkward grins. Mrs. Blum gave her a teeny smile of encouragement. Juniper wondered if Mrs. Blum had gotten in trouble too for allowing fortune telling to take place in her class.

She took her seat and organized her textbook, folder, and pen on her desk, while trying to catch a glance at Caitlin Greeley across the aisle. Caitlin's head was down, her hair hiding her face like a curtain. Juniper wanted to grab that hair and yank with every fiber in her body. This was just as much Caitlin's fault as anyone's. Asking so innocently to see the book, like she was really interested—then spreading her mother's lies! Maybe if she hadn't held it in her hot little hands, this nightmare wouldn't be taking place. Juniper trembled as she breathed in, trying to get control. She felt like a dragon ready to spit flames.

Mrs. Blum started class, pretending nothing was wrong. Since book reports were over, they diagrammed sentences. Juniper was glad. That took some real thinking, and it would keep her mind off her anger.

Someone poked her in the back and passed a note toward her. It was folded in a fancy triangle with Juniper's name spelled in colorful balloon letters. She opened it up and knew immediately it was from Nicole.

So what happend yesterday? I hope you aren't in any real trouble. My mom thinks your mom's a real pistol. Let me know before I bust!

Juniper slid the note under her folder to hide it from sight. *Tell Nicole? No way.* She wasn't about to supply the Snotty Twins with more ammo. Instead, she jumped straight to the lesson and diagrammed sentences until her fingers cramped.

When the class ended, Juniper rushed out and buried herself in the flow of students trolling aimlessly to their next class. She tried to be invisible, but she felt eyes shining on her all morning. *Will this ever stop?* When lunch came, she couldn't face the cafeteria crowd—especially Kyle Morgan, who she was sure would be sitting with Anne again. She bypassed them all, heading straight to the library.

A class of sixth graders were milling around looking for books. Juniper caught Mrs. Thompson near the back, helping one student locate a particular title. Juniper approached quietly.

"Mrs. Thompson, may I eat lunch in your back room today? I could do some work for you at the same time . . . you know, like putting labels on the new books." She held her breath, afraid Mrs.

Thompson would throw her back to the cafeteria wolves.

"I never turn down an offer for help." She winked. "I'm overwhelmed with a mountain of new books that need spine labels."

Juniper smiled at her as she let out a silent sigh of relief. Mrs. Thompson gave her the labels, and Juniper sat on the floor in the library storage room, a stack of novels by her side and a cardboard box for her lunch table. She spread out her cheese sandwich, fruit, and juice box.

Her mind relaxed into alphabetical order as she peeled and stuck labels according to the authors' last names. She didn't hear Mrs. Thompson come up behind her. When she spoke, Juniper jumped, her heart gagging her throat.

"Sorry," Mrs. Thompson said. "I thought you heard me come in."

Juniper smiled up at her. "Don't worry about it. Everything is making me jumpy these days."

"I understand. I would say you've gotten yourself into a pickle, but you seem to have dived headfirst into the whole barrel." Mrs. Thompson's voice was soft and soothing.

"I wish I could take it all back," Juniper said.

Mrs. Thompson knelt down and seated herself by Juniper. "You shouldn't feel bad. You did what you were asked to do. You simply did the assignment given."

"Which has now ticked off most everyone in school!"

"Not everyone, Juniper. Certainly not me. Do you know where those Psychic Circle books are right now?"

Juniper didn't. She shook her head.

"On the shelf in the juvenile fiction section."

Juniper registered a moment of shock. *Could this be true?*

"Don't look so surprised," Mrs. Thompson said. "I'm the school media specialist. It's my job to determine what should and shouldn't go on the shelves of my library. And I took an oath to uphold the First Amendment."

"So you don't think there is anything wrong with them?" Juniper couldn't believe what she was hearing.

"There are very few books that have something wrong with them. What's wrong for one person is fine for another. My job is to determine age appropriateness, and if the content of the book is suitable for middle-school students. I can't keep something off the shelves simply because it conflicts with someone's religion or opinion. That's why the library is full of books for every taste."

Juniper felt good hearing this. She *was* on the verge of going to the clinic after lunch to fake being sick so she could go home. The thought of trudging through the rest of the school day had hung on her like a heavy chain. But Mrs. Thompson had given her some hope. She took the last bite of her sandwich and asked, "Aren't you afraid you'll get in trouble too?"

Mrs. Thompson grinned. "I already am. Mr. Chapman threatened my job if I put those books on the shelf before the school board meeting."

"Then why did you do it?" Juniper asked, thinking Mrs. Thompson was just asking for trouble.

"I told you before. I took an oath. I told Mr. Chapman he could fire me if he wanted to, but those books would remain on the shelf until the school board rules that they can't be there."

"Boy, you're certainly brave," Juniper said.

"So are you," Mrs. Thompson assured her. "And you're not alone. We're in this together."

Juniper nodded, feeling even more relieved. She had finished her lunch as well as labeling a good amount of books. "Sorry I don't have time to shelve these for you," she said.

Mrs. Thompson shrugged. "I have parent volunteers to help me out there. Don't worry about it."

Juniper rose and picked up her trash. Before she walked away, Mrs. Thompson said, "Juniper, I wouldn't be a very good librarian if I didn't assign you some research."

"After I did all this work for you? Gee, thanks a lot."

Mrs. Thompson grinned. "This is research you'll enjoy. Before the board meeting next week, I'd like you to look up information on censorship and banned books."

Juniper cocked an eyebrow toward her. "That's easy. I'd planned to do it anyway."

CHAPTER 6

Nowhere to Hide

After school, Anne and Gena caught up with Juniper as she was unlocking her bike from the rack.

"Just ignore us, why don't you?" Anne said, looking pouty.

Juniper looked around at them. "Sorry. My head seems to be up in space these days."

"Better in space than full of space," Gena said with a goofy giggle. "Like Anne's."

"Look who's talking," Anne argued.

Gena stopped fooling with her lock and gave Anne a dead-on look. "What? I'm not the one going out with Booger Boy."

"Shut up," Anne said. "He's not so bad."

Juniper pulled the chains from her spokes and asked the dreaded question. "Did he trash me much at lunch today?"

Anne shied away, but Gena answered. "A little."

"And you guys did speak up for me, right?"

"Of course," Gena said, her voice positive and sure. Anne fooled with her bike.

"What did he say?" Juniper asked, although she wasn't sure she really wanted to know.

Before Gena could answer, Anne busted in, "Look, it's not that big a deal. He just doesn't think like us. Is that a crime?"

Juniper thought about her conversation with Mrs. Thompson and how everyone had different tastes and opinions.

Gena straddled her bike and popped it from the rack. "It's a crime to make up lies. And that's what he's doing."

Anne pulled her bike away too. "Whatever. I'm leaving."

"Me too," Juniper said. "I have dance class tonight."

★ ★ ★

Juniper pedaled up to her driveway, stopped suddenly, and froze. It appeared as though a dairy truck had exploded on the garage door. Eggs were splattered in firework patterns and something else had oozed and dried on its way down. Ice cream? Yogurt? It didn't matter. What mattered was someone had done this simply because of her book report.

"Mom!" Juniper called, racing into the kitchen. "Someone egged our house!"

"Awesome," Jonathan said, dashing away from the kitchen table and scattering his homework as he went.

Juniper's mom shook her head. "I thought I heard noises out front." She walked out too.

Juniper followed, wondering what her mom would do now. *My mom thinks your mom's a real pistol,* Nicole had written. But just what would it take before she really fired away?

"Look at this mess," Mom said. "I'm just glad the car was inside the garage." She paused as though taking it all in. "Who would do such a thing?"

"I bet it was Stephen West," Jonathan said. "Today at recess he and Kerry Morgan called me a devil worshiper and said I was going to hell. Then they said my sister was Goth, and my whole family would perish in flames."

"I'm not Goth!" Juniper shouted.

Mom raised her hand for calm, but Juniper could see it trembling. She wondered how long her mom could keep control. "You know, Jonathan," Mom said. "Those are big words coming from nine-year-olds. Sounds like they heard it from somewhere else. Most likely their parents."

"Or brothers," Juniper added. "Kerry Morgan's brother Kyle is in my English class. But he thinks it's all bunk, not devil worship."

"Just please try to ignore the other kids when they say things," Mom said. "We are going to state our case to the school board at the meeting next Monday night. Let's not fuel the flames before then."

"Which flames?" Juniper asked. "The ones we're supposed to perish in?"

Mom came over and gave her a hug. She squeezed tightly, and Juniper welcomed the secure feeling. She couldn't help but wonder, *If I'm so gifted in fortune telling, then why didn't I see all this coming?*

★　★　★

Juniper dressed for dance class, although she really wished she didn't have to go. She wanted to stay hidden in her house forever. If the boys in fourth grade were teasing Jonathan, then the whole town must know by now. Maybe they could move to a new town—just slip away in the night while everyone was asleep. It was the only solution. That or staying locked in her room until the next century. But instead of curling up in a corner to rot, Juniper put on her black cut-off capris and a black tee shirt with the name of her dance studio, Sugar Babies. She picked up the pendulum from her dresser and slipped it under her bed pillow. She wanted it there for safe keeping and, hopefully, for answers to the nightmare in her dreams.

As usual, Mom dropped Juniper off first, then headed on to Jonathan's baseball practice. She grabbed the door handle of the dance studio, but as soon as Mom drove away, Juniper made a dash into the tanning salon next door. She sat on a waiting room chair and hid behind a fashion magazine, pretending to read.

"Can I help you?" a teenage girl asked, her skin tanned as toast.

Juniper peered up over the magazine and forced a grin. "I'm just hiding out for a few minutes. Is that okay?"

"It depends on who you're hiding from," the toasty girl answered. "You're not going to get me in any trouble, are you? Because I just started working here last week."

Probably, Juniper wanted to say. *I've been nothing but bad news lately.* "I'm only staying for five minutes," she assured the worried girl. "Just until my dance class starts."

Miss Toasty shrugged and went back to her counter and the phone conversation that Juniper had obviously interrupted. *And she's worried about me getting her into trouble!*

She flipped through the pages in the magazine while her knee quivered like an earthquake. It wasn't until Miss toasty stopped her phone conversation again and stared that Juniper realized her nervous twitch was rumbling the entire area. She tossed the magazine back on the coffee table and left.

Her timing was good. The class had already started their warm-ups when Juniper rushed in, pretending to be late. She took her place on the floor for stretches. With her head on her knees, she looked right. Everyone on that side was looking straight at her, their cheeks resting on knees.

She switched to the left—same thing only vice versa. At least she didn't have to talk to them; that was the whole reason for coming in late.

Nicole Hoffman tried to whisper to her several times, but Juniper pretended not to hear. She'd shrug and point to Shug Ellerbe, the dance teacher, with body language suggesting they should pay attention.

But once they got into the real dancing, Juniper found herself caught up in the combinations and lost herself in the music. Dancing was as important to her as eating and sleeping. She couldn't imagine a life without it. And those forty-five minutes were the best she'd had in the last couple of days.

When class ended, Juniper snapped back to reality and headed straight for the door, not even bothering to change out of her jazz shoes first. She wasn't quite quick enough. "Are you going to tell me what's going on or not?" Nicole asked, grabbing Juniper's arm.

"Not," Juniper said in a nice voice. "Not now. My mom's waiting," she lied. She scooted out the door as quickly as her feet would fly, and circled back into the tanning salon. Miss Toasty slumped when she saw her.

Juniper stood by the glass door and watched until her mom drove up. She made a run for it to the car, before anyone else could stop her to talk.

"What were you doing over there?" Mom asked.

Juniper thought up a good fib, but Mom could always see through a lie. "Hiding," she said. "I'm not in the mood to socialize."

"Well, I'm in the mood to eat," Jonathan announced, his voice loud and shrill. "Can we go to Dairy Treat now? I'm starving!"

Mom steered the car onto the street. "Try not to wilt in the next ten minutes and I'll get you there."

Juniper thought of a sarcastic remark about Jonathan wilting, but decided it was best not to start anything. It seemed her family was the only ones on her side. And Gena. She wasn't sure about Anne. Her stomach filled with sour juices just thinking about Anne and Kyle Morgan. But she shoved the thought away. After all, she did want to enjoy her cheeseburger tonight.

They turned into the driveway of the Dairy Treat and parked up front. But no one got out of the car. No one spoke. And Juniper was ready to slump down in the seat and disappear. There by the front door was a card table manned by three women—Mrs. Greeley, Mrs. Morgan, and another lady Juniper didn't recognize. The banner hanging from the front of the table read:

SUPPORT GOODNESS.
DRIVE EVIL OUT OF AVERY!

CHAPTER 7

Message Received

"Drive evil out of Avery?'" Jonathan said, half reading, half questioning.

Juniper could practically see the smoke fumes coming from her mother's face. "I'll drive all right," Mom said, racing the car engine. "I'll drive this car right over those busy body bi—"

"Mom!" Juniper said, clutching the steering wheel. "Let's just go."

"But I'm hungry!" Jonathan argued. "Let's go to the drive-through."

Juniper didn't take her eyes off her mom, who still glared straight ahead. *Is it possible for someone to start a fire simply by staring at someone?*

"Mom," Juniper pleaded. "Let's just go."

"Let's eat," Jonathan whined.

Mom didn't say anything. Juniper thought she was hyperventilating. Her knuckles were bone white, clutching the steering wheel. To make matters worse, the ladies behind the card table were staring back. Even Sweetums was looking at them from the front pack Mrs. Greeley wore. Juniper imagined the dog's lilac scent overpowering the smell of the burgers.

"They have no right," Mom said in a near whisper.

"Yes, they do," Juniper said. "Remember that stuff about the First Amendment? Freedom of speech and all that?"

This seemed to snap Mom out of ballistic mode. She took a deep breath and exhaled it like a warped balloon.

Right then, Mrs. Wilson, Beth's mom, came out of Dairy Treat holding two bags, her purse, and her car keys. Juniper leaned forward, anxious to see what a Snotty Twin mom would do.

"Come sign our petition," Mrs. Greeley said, obviously speaking loud and clear for the Lynches' sake.

To Juniper's surprise, Mrs. Wilson smiled and shook her head. She bobbed out to her car, juggling her take-out, got in, and drove away.

So where did Beth inherit her snottiness from?

Jonathan leaned over to the front seat. "We're going to drive through now, right?"

"Wrong," Mom said, backing up. "We're going somewhere that doesn't support these buffoons." In a calm easy manner, she drove out into the darkness.

Fifteen silent minutes later, she pulled into the Village and the parking lot of Food For Thought.

The restaurant looked quiet and dim, not at all like it was on weekends. But Juniper could sit up straight here. The Village was a block of New Age shops, and Food For Thought catered to the health nuts—New Age health nuts who wouldn't burn someone at the stake for doing a little fortune telling demo.

"These are the worst French fries in the world," Jonathan said, picking at his food.

"They're not French fries, they're potato skins," Mom corrected.

Jonathan peeled one in half and held it up. "Last time we were here you told me they were French fries."

Mom lowered his arm so he'd drop the skin back on the plate. "I only told you that so you'd eat them."

"Are these real chicken nuggets?" he asked.

"Just eat," Mom said, cutting into her chef salad.

But Juniper didn't feel like eating. In Mrs. Greeley's attempt to drive evil out, she'd also driven Juniper's hunger away.

"We'll win this," Mom said, patting Juniper's hand.

Juniper managed to hold back the tears that had been building all day. "I don't want to win."

"What?" Mom said, dropping her fork beside her salad bowl. "You don't want to win?"

Juniper shook her head. "No. I don't want to win. I want to settle. I want everything to be normal. I want them to back off and for everybody to pretend nothing happened."

Mom brushed a wisp of hair from Juniper's face. "Let me handle this, okay?"

Juniper stayed quiet. She couldn't tell her mom what she really thought: that Mom might screw everything up badly. That she might get suspended. That after tonight, she didn't think she'd be able to face the kids and teachers at Avery Middle School ever again.

"This chicken nugget has a big vein in it!" Jonathan spouted.

Mom took it from his hand and dropped it back onto his plate. "It's a slice of red pepper."

"Gross!"

Yep, Juniper thought. *That's exactly how I feel right now.*

Juniper trailed into the house and headed for her room. She could hear Mom starting in, telling Dad what happened.

"Juniper," Dad called to her, interrupting the "drive evil out of Avery" story. "Anne called twice for you. Sounds urgent."

Juniper nodded and kept walking. If Anne needed her urgently, then chances were the emergency had to do with the book report. She didn't think she could handle another moment of that tonight. She was on the brink anyway, and one little push could send her over. She decided not to call Anne back, opening her email instead. Naturally, there was a message from Anne, a.k.a. Cheer_N_Diva.

> Hey girl! I need you to call me. I've found a new form of divination that is awesome! This calls for a FTC meeting ASAP.
>
> A.

What a relief. Something normal for a change. She certainly could use a Fortune Tellers Club meeting. Before hitting reply, she noticed a message from Gena also.

Check out the community message board.

Juniper clicked on the link and brought up the Avery community page. The message board, usually filled with lost dog rewards and bridge club announcements, had an unusual message at the very top. The subject header had a familiar ring.

DRIVE EVIL OUT OF AVERY!

Against her better judgment, Juniper clicked on it.

Good citizens of Avery,

As you are all well aware, our middle school was recently polluted by a foul ritual performed in one of the classrooms. This ritual included fortune telling, witchcraft, and other blasphemes disguised behind the mask of a so-called book report. Many of you know the family of the young woman who conducted this indecent rite, particularly the mother, who has from time to time corrupted the neighborhood with tea leaf readings, spreading this disease and brainwashing youth and adults alike. I personally believe this is the work of a cult. This family and their young daughter should be made to repent before all our children are delivered into the hands of Satan. That is why I'm asking each of you to sign a petition that will be delivered to the school board on Monday night. Help me clean up the community for good.

—Gayle Greeley

Tears did flow now, but this time from anger. Juniper felt a volcano slowly erupting in her stomach, and the lava flowing upward into her throat. How dare Mrs. Greeley! It was tough enough when the attacks were on her, but Juniper couldn't sit back and let this loudmouthed woman talk badly about her mom. A cult? Get real.

With shaky fingers, Juniper clicked on another message she saw below that. The subject read:

Do You Have Bats For Brains?

Dear Mrs. Greeley (if that is your real name), I happen to know the family and the "young woman" you are referring to. She is really a sweet person who wouldn't hurt anyone even if her own butt was on the line. And I know her mother too, and she's super cool, and she didn't brainwash me to say that. So I suggest you take your petition, roll it up nice and tight, and shove it up your . . . nose.

Sincerely, G. R. Picklesworth III,
upstanding Avery citizen

Juniper laughed even though she was touched deeply by the posting. G. R. Picklesworth III? *Where did Gena come up with that name?* She wiped her streaming tears and runny nose with the back of her hand and settled back to the computer screen. She could only imagine the fireworks when Mom read Mrs. Greeley's message. It was definitely time to take action—fast!

She clicked the mouse on a search engine and typed in "banned books." She started with the first link. *Holy bananas! Was this a joke?*

CHAPTER 8

Marble Magic

Juniper rolled over and opened her eyes. *Ugh!* Her alarm was set to go off in ten minutes. *Should I just stay here or get up?* The idea of lying in bed all day appealed to her, but she knew better. She'd get up, get dressed, and face another day of painful gawks and stares, and maybe more, at Avery Middle School.

She reached under the pillow and retrieved the pendulum. It felt cold to the touch, but still comforting. She really wished she could wear it around her neck at school. It could double as an amulet, warding off negative energy. But it'd probably cause more problems than it would solve.

She rolled out of bed, shut off the alarm, and dragged herself across the room like she had an anchor attached to her—that's how it felt, anyway. This week had certainly weighed her down. She opened *Grave Dangers* and plopped the pendulum across the open page like a bookmark. Closing it back up, she headed into the kitchen for some breakfast.

★　★　★

"So? Did you see the community bulletin board?" Gena asked.

Juniper was in no mood to talk about it. "Yep . . . thanks," she said softly.

Gena looked sympathetic for a moment, then put on a bossy expression. "You're not actually going to let this suck you down the drain, are you?"

Juniper didn't speak, but Gena was right. That's exactly what was happening.

"Get real! That woman is a fruitcake deluxe—extra nuts. She's not going to win."

Juniper shrugged. She refused to talk about it. Luckily, Anne came running up, interrupting them.

"Did you get my email about the new fortune telling method I contrived?" she asked, grinning like she'd just won the Nobel Prize. "Wait till you see how it works!"

"Tell us now," Gena insisted.

"No time." Anne was huffing and out of breath. "I've got to go in and meet the other cheerleaders for a short meeting. I'm late." She jogged away, then looked back over her shoulders. "This afternoon! Juniper's house, as usual."

"Well, that should perk you up," Gena said. "Anne's going to solve all your problems. I have a feeling her prophesies will help you chill out."

Juniper worked up a smile. "I need every inch of help I can get. After all, I don't have a petition like Mrs. Greeley."

"Nope," Gena said. "You have something better. Common sense."

★   ★   ★

By the end of the day, Juniper was in a much better mood. No one had given her dirty looks or made snippy comments. And the biggest surprise was a note passed to her.

It was Nicole's handwriting.

Juniper, I'm on your side

It almost made her feel guilty for calling Nicole a Snotty Twin . . . almost.

When she got home, Jonathan was sprawled out in front of the TV. "Hope you're happy," he said. His mouth puckered like he'd been sucking a lemon.

Juniper smiled. "I am."

"Because of you, half my friends aren't speaking to me."

Juniper smiled even bigger. "Then they weren't really your friends, were they?"

Jonathan crossed his arms and focused his eyes on the television. Juniper strolled off to her room.

She gathered up the info she'd printed off the Web last night, then opened *Grave Dangers* for her pendulum. When she picked it up, the book came with it. *Huh?* The plastic green circle had stuck to the page. Juniper carefully peeled it away, but bits of paper and print came with it. She couldn't imagine what caused it to stick like that. Had Jonathan been messing around in here? The pendulum had left three tiny holes in the page. And those torn bits were still on it. One contained the word "may." Another read "three years," and the other fragment said "newspaper."

Juniper started to peel them off, then stopped. Was the pendulum trying to tell her something? She shrugged it off. *I've got to get my mind on something else!* Slipping the pendulum around her neck, she opened her homework.

★ ★ ★

Anne and Gena came in together. Anne was holding something that looked like a bag of marbles.

"What is that, runes?" Juniper asked, excited over the chance to try something new.

"You'll see," Anne said, settling on the floor.

Gena threw up her hands. "I've asked a million and three times, coming over here. Her lips are sealed . . . with cement!"

Anne gave Gena a look. "I just didn't want to explain it twice, comprendé?"

"Whatever," Gena said. "Just show us!"

Anne opened the bag and laid out a rectangular piece of pink felt that she'd marked with a large X. In each quadrant of the X she'd written a different word: past, present, future, outcome.

"Like reading tarot," Juniper said.

Then Anne dumped out twelve sparkling glass marbles—only these were oval with flat bottoms, each a different brilliant color.

Gena scooted closer into the circle. "Cool. Where'd you get those?"

"At the craft store. There were bins and bins of them. They're supposed to be used for holding up flower arrangements, but the minute I saw them, I had a better idea." She gathered up the marbles, then handed them to Juniper. "Each one is the same as a birthstone color . . . except they only had one type of red, so I bought a black one for garnet. Now hold them over the felt, concentrate on what you want to know, and drop them."

Juniper closed her eyes. She thought about the situation at school, Mrs. Greeley, and the school board meeting next Monday night. She tried to visualize them without concocting her own outcome to the problem. As she steadied her focus, her arms lightly tingled. Focusing on the problem, she dropped the marbles and opened her eyes.

Only seven of them landed on the rectangle. One in the past. Three in the present. Two in the future. One fell on the line between past and outcome. The girls leaned in.

Anne unfolded a piece of paper. "We interpret it by the color meanings that I printed off the Internet last night. So let's start with the past . . . the amethyst."

"But it's not really an amethyst," Gena said. "It's a purple marble."

"Right," Anne continued, "but it represents an amethyst."

Juniper wiggled where she sat. "So what does the paper say?"

Anne ran her finger down the list. "Amethyst: dreams, psychic abilities, meditation."

Juniper exhaled some pent-up breath. "That makes sense. It's the past, so it's referring to the book report. Go on to the present."

Anne checked her list again. "The sapphire . . . or blue marble," she said to Gena, "represents magic or power."

"Whoa!" Gena said, scootching back some. "Black magic?"

Juniper suddenly felt chilled. "I hope not."

Anne held her hand up. "Let's check out the meanings of the other marbles first, then try to fit it together." She tapped the black marble. "This means healing or protection."

"So I'm being protected from black magic?" Juniper asked.

"Maybe," Anne said. "Let's see what the turquoise means. Nature, luck, or immediate answers."

"Ahem," Gena said, sitting tall. "Let's recap the present, shall we? We've got some powerful magic being thrown Juniper's way for which she needs immediate answers to protect herself."

Juniper shrugged. "Why not? Sounds good to me." She glanced at the two marbles cradled against each other in the future quadrant. "I guess it's safe to say these meanings are connected."

"What's this yellow one?" Gena asked.

Anne looked up from her page. "Topaz. It means healing or communication. And the light green marble means luck."

"That's good," Juniper said, hoping she was right.

Anne nodded. "Either you'll get lucky, or you'll need all the luck you can get."

"Thanks a lot!"

"Or . . ." Gena said, "It could mean you'll get some good news."

"That would be nice," Juniper said. "This red marble is lying on the line. How do you interpret that?"

Anne checked. "Well, it means love, emotion, or passion."

"Whose?" Gena asked.

Juniper wondered if the marble was lying on the line because the outcome was somehow connected to the past. But how? She looked again at the yellow marble that represented communication. That reminded her of the banned book research she'd done last night. The pendulum grew warm as she sorted through the possibilities of the reading.

"I think I know a better way to understand all this," she said. She slipped her hand under the collar of her tee shirt and brought out the pendulum. "I bet the answers lie here."

CHAPTER 9

Negotiating

Gena laughed. "The answers are in that? I thought that was just for solving Psychic Circle mysteries."

"We're kinda like the Psychic Circle," Anne said. "Look how many times we've used fortune telling to get through our problems."

Juniper held up the pendulum, showing the side with the bits of paper stuck on it. "Take a look at this."

Anne and Gena leaned in, squinting toward the tiny type. "What's that all about?" Gena asked.

Juniper wished she knew. "I'm not sure. These are words that stuck to the pendulum when I was taking it out of the book. They must mean something." She slipped the pendulum off and laid it down between them.

Gena let out an uneven whistle. "This makes about as much sense as Anne's marbles."

Juniper had hoped something would snap right away—that Gena or Anne or even she would suddenly have all the answers. But stuck-on paper and floral marbles weren't sending the vibes she needed. It was going to take some logic, luck, and mega-interpretation. "Think of it as a code," Juniper said. "Combined with the marble reading, we could find the answers."

"One of the words is *may*," Anne said. "Is it saying we *may* do something?"

"Yeah," Gena said. "But when? I mean, we may do something three years from now."

Juniper went on studying the words, her focus going back and forth from the pendulum to the marbles. An idea struck. *Duh!* She picked up the pendulum and held it over the felt. An electric tingle purred through her arm. The pendulum didn't swing. Instead, it jerked like a magnet, pulling furiously. And with a *flumph,* it popped loose from her fingers and fell on the yellow marble, fitting around it perfectly.

Anne and Gena both stared, eyes lit. Gena's mouth gaped. "Should I scream now or wait to see if anything creepier happens? Because I think that was creepy-maximus."

Anne picked up the plastic piece. The yellow marble stayed stuck within. "Maybe we should report this to *Ripley's Believe It Or Not!*"

"They probably wouldn't believe it either," Gena said.

Juniper believed it. With all her heart. Yellow—communication. There was a message there. A message to communicate. She took the circle from Anne and clutched it like a jewel. "I think I know what I'm suppose to do."

★ ★ ★

"This is insane," Anne said as they pedaled their bikes around the corner.

Juniper didn't even glance at Anne. She kept her eyes focused on the road and her mind focused on what she'd say. "What's insane is that I didn't think of it before."

Gena caught up to Juniper. "It's not going to work. That lady is loco."

Juniper slowed her pace a bit. Maybe it wouldn't work, but she had to try. She didn't bother to answer Gena. Minutes later, they pulled into the Greeley's driveway.

"Are you sure about this?" Anne asked.

"No," Juniper said. "But what harm can it do?"

Gena stopped, grabbing Juniper's arm and jerking her back. "Maybe Anne and I should wait here?"

"Why are you afraid? And besides, what's she going to do, conk us with her Bible?"

"Hey, that's one big book," Gena said. "It could hurt."

Juniper grabbed Gena by the hem of her tee shirt. "Come on, Miss G. R. Picklesworth III."

Juniper ignored the doorbell and rapped lightly on the door. She'd barely lifted her fist away when she heard *Yip! Yip! Yip!* Sweetums was scratching on the other side of the door.

"Beware of attack dog," Anne said.

"Are you talking about the pooch or Mrs. Greeley?" Gena asked.

The door opened and Caitlin Greeley peered out, looking dumbstruck and frightened. Sweetums tried to bounce out, but Caitlin blocked his way with her foot. She shut the door partway, leaving a slight opening. "Juniper, you shouldn't be here," she whispered.

Juniper breathed in the lilac air. "I'd like to speak to your mom."

"No." Caitlin's voice was soft, but her tone was stern.

A voice drifted from a back room. "Who is it, Caitlin?"

"Nobody!" Her voice returned to a panicked murmur. "Go!"

Juniper looked at Anne and Gena. They both stood still, eyeing Caitlin. Maybe this was a bad idea.

"Please," Caitlin begged.

The distant voice grew closer. "Is it someone to sign the petition?" The door flung open and there stood Mrs. Greeley, taking up most of the entrance. "What do you want?"

"I just came to talk to you."

Mrs. Greeley crossed her arms, making her appear another foot taller. She pushed Caitlin out of the way, much the same as Caitlin had blocked Sweetums. "I think it's too late for apologies, don't you?"

That caught Juniper off guard for a moment. "No . . . uh . . . wait. I didn't come to apologize."

"Figures," Mrs. Greeley said, her face tight as a rubber band. "Does your mama know you're here?"

"No, ma'am."

Mrs. Greeley flashed her perfect white teeth. "Not much of a tea leaf reader then, huh?"

Juniper refrained from rolling her eyes. This woman didn't know diddly about reading tea leaves . . . or any divination for that matter. *How*

can you challenge something you know nothing about?
"I just thought maybe we could settle things now."

"We'll settle them on Monday night."

Juniper didn't get another word in before Mrs. Greeley slammed the door in her face. She'd never been treated so badly before, at least not by an adult. She should have been angry herself, but instead, she was hurt. She took a deep breath to hold in her tears.

"That went well," Anne said.

Gena snickered. "Yeah. At least she didn't pound us with her Bible."

Juniper got on her bike and coasted away. She briefly glanced back, seeing Caitlin peeking through the blinds.

CHAPTER 10

The Top Ten

Juniper crept up the driveway, pushing her bike by hand. She'd said goodbye to Gena and Anne down at the corner, and now had high hopes of sneaking into the house without much fuss from anyone. As she quietly clicked open the front door, the smell of greasy fried chicken clung to the air. Take-out food . . . again. Before stepping in, she heard her mom and dad in the kitchen.

"It's outrageous!" Mom cried. "First the community board, now the newspaper. This woman is too much!"

"Calm down, Joy." Dad's voice was stern but soft. "You'll get your blood pressure up."

"It's already up. This woman is plain vicious, and I plan to do something about it Monday night."

Juniper heard Dad's chair scrape the linoleum. "I thought this dispute was about the First Amendment, not revenge on Gayle Greeley."

"But she's attacked Juniper twice now. Think of our daughter."

"I am thinking of her," Dad said. "And the last thing she needs is you going off the deep end."

Juniper had heard enough. She made some extra-warning noises walking in and headed for the kitchen. "Sorry I'm late."

Mom and Dad both sat at the table. Neither smiled, although Dad nodded.

"Where were you?" Jonathan asked, gravy dotting his chin.

"What's it to you?" Juniper said.

Mom sipped some iced tea and looked at Juniper. "We'd all like to know."

"Just riding around." Okay—so it was a half lie.

They went back to their food. Juniper glanced at Mom, savagely ripping into her chicken wing, flinging bits of crust all over her plate. Had she ever been this riled before?

Juniper ate. She barely tasted the chicken though. All her senses were focused on the dumb mistake she'd made just minutes earlier. *What was I thinking? Mrs. Greeley was a stubborn old busybody. I should have known better than to go over there.* She went about her meal silently, feeling like a castaway on a deflating raft.

Before getting up, Juniper saw the newspaper on the kitchen counter. She didn't want to read what Mrs. Greeley had put in it. She felt miserable enough as it was. But the sight of the newspaper triggered the pendant. It heated to a pleasant warmth, like a cuddly blanket or some fuzzy slippers. *Newspaper.* That was one of the words stuck to the pendulum . . . and undoubtedly an answer to her problem.

She went back to her room and closed the door. Pulling the pendant out, she looked at the words again. *Newspaper. Three years. May.* She grabbed the phone and quickly dialed, but before she hit the last digit, someone knocked at her door.

"Jonathan, go away!"

Dad stuck his head in. "You know, you really should be nicer to your brother."

Juniper hung up the phone. "Sorry."

Dad slipped in and shut the door.

"Is something wrong?" Juniper asked.

Dad sat down on the edge of her bed. "You tell me."

Is everyone in this family psychic? "I'm fine, Dad."

He nodded. "Good. Because your mom . . . well . . . you know how she gets when she's got a cause."

My mom thinks your mom's a real pistol. "I think everyone knows," Juniper said.

"Just don't let this business get you down too much. If you want to talk, you can always count on me." He leaned over and kissed her forehead. Only a faint trace of his aftershave lingered, but the familiar smell always made her feel safe. "We love you," he said.

He sprang up from the bed and headed for the door.

"What's her deal?" Juniper asked just before Dad walked out.

"What?"

"Mrs. Greeley. What's her deal?"

Dad smiled and winked. "She's just trying to rid the world of evil forces."

"Then maybe she should catch the first rocket to Mars."

Dad chuckled. "Yep. What's the saying about glass houses?" He quietly closed the door.

Juniper dialed the phone again. She got the answering machine. It was Gena's voice. "You've reached the Richmond residence. At the beep please leave a message. A good message. You know, like Dad won the lottery or a trip for two to Hawaii. Be sure to speak clearly. However, if you are the bearer of bad news, this tape will self-destruct at the tone."

Beeeep.

Juniper rushed the message. "Gena? Don't make any plans for after school tomorrow. We're heading for the library."

★ ★ ★

"Could you explain that again?" Gena asked as she leaned against the magnolia before school.

"We're going to the library," Juniper said. "For research."

Gena held up her hand. "It's Friday. We have no book reports due. No social studies assignments. Not even 'What You Did Over Summer Vacation.' And you expect me to spend a lovely Friday afternoon at the library doing research?"

"What kind of research?" Anne asked, talking as though Gena didn't exist.

"We're going to look up something in an old newspaper."

Anne's eyes turned to slits, and Gena stood up straight. They both spoke at once, but Anne beat Gena to the question. "What are we looking up?"

Juniper was hesitant to answer. What *were* they looking up? "I'm not sure," she said. "I just know that the answer to this nightmare is in the newspaper. Look at this." She opened the front zipper of her backpack and pulled out the paper she'd printed from the Internet. "These are the top ten most challenged books last year. People wanted these books banned."

The girls leaned in to look. *"Huckleberry Finn!"* Gena said. "What's wrong with that book? Isn't it just about a couple of guys who go rafting?"

Juniper pointed to the explanation. "Says here, because of racial sensitivity. You do know we have to read that book in high school."

"I've read it already," Anne said.

Juniper looked up at Anne. She knew Anne enjoyed reading, but she never pegged her for someone who'd choose Huck Finn.

"It's because of an ugly slur word that was common back in Mark Twain's day," Anne said. "It's used a lot in that book."

"I saw the movie," Gena said. "They didn't use any ugly words in it."

"Have you ever seen a movie that's the same as the book?" Juniper asked.

Gena shrugged. "If I'm going to see the movie, then why read the book?"

"Oh, pleeeeeeease," Juniper said. "Look what else is listed. *A Bridge to Terabithia.*"

"What?" Gena turned the paper around for a better look. "I did read that one."

"We all did," Anne said. "In fifth grade."

"But check out one of the reasons," Juniper said.

Anne nearly tore the paper, jerking it toward her. "No way!"

"What?" Gena asked, grabbing at it.

Juniper tilted her head toward Gena and whispered, "Occultism and Satanism."

Gena's mouth dropped into an *O*. "Guess I missed that part."

"Who wants to ban these books anyway?" Anne asked, her eyes scanning the paper up and down.

Juniper knew. She knew full well. "People like Mrs. Greeley. You know, trying to rid the world of evil forces."

The bell rang and Juniper tucked the paper back into her pack. "This afternoon, guys. The library."

CHAPTER 11

Extra! Extra!

Juniper was actually looking forward to first period. She wanted to talk to Caitlin. She wasn't going to let her skulk back and hide behind her hair either. Caitlin was going to answer a few choice questions. But five minutes into the class, it was evident that she wouldn't get her answers. Caitlin was absent. *Figures. Just as well,* Juniper thought. *It might have only made things worse.*

She made it through the day with only minimal stares from other students. Who cares about serious issues on Friday anyway? Juniper headed out the side door to her bike. She spotted Anne at the bike rack already . . . with Kyle Morgan. *Ugh!* Juniper could see that their discussion was intense, even though she couldn't hear what they were arguing about. They both became strangely quiet when Juniper approached.

"You ready to go?" Juniper asked, fidgeting with the combination on her bike lock.

"As soon as Gena gets here," Anne answered.

Kyle stepped in between them. "You said you'd go to the video store with me."

"That was *before,* Kyle." Anne draped her backpack on her handlebars.

"Before what? Tell me!"

Juniper pretended to unlock her bike, not wanting to hurry. She intended to stay as far away from this squabble as possible.

"Before Juniper needed my help," Anne said.

Kyle kicked the dirt with the toe of his sneaker. A cloud of it hit Juniper's arm. So much for staying far away. "Watch out!" she said, pushing his leg back.

Kyle's eyes were like flames ready to explode. "*You* watch out! You're the one who's in trouble, not me. You're the one who's causing problems at school. You're the one who's gonna fry on Monday night!" He turned to Anne. "You might as well go with me to the video store. I'm the one who'll be around next week. Not Freaky here, who's about to get expelled."

"We'll *all* be here," Anne said. "The difference is, you'll be the one without a girlfriend."

Gena had come up just in time to hear Anne's breakup. "Cool. Guess it's just *snot* meant to be, Booger Boy," she said.

Kyle shoved Gena aside and stomped away.

"I'm going to miss him," Gena said with a giggle.

Anne didn't say anything. Juniper could tell she was hurt, maybe even a bit wounded. She stared at the ground with every movement she made. Juniper hated being the one to come between them, but just like Gena's message on the community board, it made her feel great to have such hardcore friends.

The wind blew roughly as they rode to the library. Juniper had had enough obstacles lately; she wasn't going to let a strong gust detour her now. They parked their bikes and entered Avery's public library.

"So where do we start?" Anne asked.

Juniper fingered the warm pendant, bringing it out in full view. She didn't bother looking at the words on it again. She knew. "We look in newspapers."

Gena turned a full 360 degrees. "Where do they keep them?"

"Good question," Juniper said.

★　★　★

"We're trying to scan and convert it all to CD-ROM," the librarian said. "But it's a long and arduous process. Most of our archives are still on microfilm."

"Microfilm? Like James Bond? 007? All that?" Gena said.

The librarian chuckled as she threaded the microfilm onto the spool. "Not quite as exciting, I'm afraid. But then, you never know what will turn up." With the click of a switch, a lighted photo of a newspaper page appeared on the screen. Crooked, but there. "You use this knob to straighten the image, and this one to view the next page." She turned a large, round dial and the film spun into a blur. It stopped on a newspaper issued a few days later.

"Thanks," Juniper said as the librarian walked away.

"So is this going to be like fortune telling?" Anne asked. "We spin the dial, concentrate, and it'll land on the exact newspaper we need?"

"Like *Wheel of Fortune*," Gena said.

Juniper sighed. "I don't think it'll be that easy." She was slightly turning the knob, getting the feel for the microfilm reader.

"What made you decide to look back three years?" Anne asked.

Juniper pointed to the words "three years" on the pendant. "Lucky guess?"

They started at the beginning of the year. "Look for anything that has to do with banned books," Juniper told them. "I bet that's our smoking gun."

They hovered together and Juniper spun the microfilm, one newspaper page at a time. After a few minutes, Gena rubbed her eyes. "Are we going to scan every newspaper on here?"

"We may have to," Juniper answered. But the moment the words left her mouth, the pendant heated to an uncomfortable prickle. Then she realized what she'd said. "We *may* have to."

"You said that," Gena pointed out.

"*May*. We *may* have to. *May!* Let's look at the newspapers in May."

Gena rolled her eyes. "Oh, great. Naturally it'll be a month with thirty-one days."

Juniper stopped and thought. The pendulum had led her this far. Surely it had all the answers. She thought about the words again. Four of them.

There were four words on the pendant. "Let's try May fourth."

She spun the dial. March eighth. Again. April twentieth. Again. May ninth. It took some extra twisting and turning till she reached the headlines of May fourth. "This is just a bunch of national news." She went to the next page, then the next. Bingo!

"This is it," Juniper said. "Look at this headline—'Avery Librarian Fights to Keep Potter on the Shelf.' Whatever is in this article will be the key to defending myself."

Juniper began reading about the heroic librarian who wouldn't let a local church group ban Harry Potter from the library. She'd barely gotten past the first paragraph when Gena tapped her shoulder . . . hard.

"Juniper, I don't think that's it."

Juniper had been annoyed with Gena plenty of times, but this time she snapped. "I'm reading!"

"Trust me, Juniper. Scroll down."

Juniper sighed, scrolled down, and the minute her eyes hit the page, her breath hung in her throat. "No way!"

"How about them headlines," Gena said with a happy smirk.

"I don't believe it!" Anne sputtered.

Juniper could barely move. She nervously focused the microfilm reader to center the article, and pushed the copy button. The page printed out for her to take. All three girls stared at the paper.

"This is so unbelievable," Anne said.

Juniper agreed. She couldn't believe her own good luck. She read the headline one more time to make sure it was real.

Pet Psychic Locates Missing Pet Owner Elated

The picture spoke as loudly as the headline. There was no mistaking the owner or her dog.

CHAPTER 12

The Verdict

J uniper read the article again after she got home. It was just too good to believe.

New Avery resident Gayle Greeley is breathing easier now that her precious little Sweetums has been returned to her. Sweetums, a one-year-old toy poodle, had been missing since last Tuesday. When search volunteers and missing posters failed to supply results, Mrs. Greeley turned to Houston Pet Psychic, Sean McNeal.

"Gayle faxed a picture of Sweetums to me, and I knew where he was within an hour of leaving Houston," McNeal stated.

Sweetums was found with eighty-one-year-old Elvin Jones, an invalid living just outside the city limits. "The little critter had no dog tag, just a fancy bow," Mr. Jones commented. "I fed him well. He likes chicken gizzards."

The reunion of Sweetums and Gayle Greeley was a joyous event. "I don't know what I'd do without my Sweetums," Mrs. Greeley told us. "He's my baby and my treasure!"

Juniper lightly folded the article and stuck it under her socks in the top drawer. Just before closing it, she took the pendulum from around her neck, and placed it on top of the paper. The pendulum would protect it until Monday night.

Several times during the weekend, Juniper thought about showing the article to her mom. But she always talked herself out of it, considering it a risk. All she needed was for Mom to rush over to the Greeley place and wave the article in Mrs. Greeley's face. Juniper figured the best thing was to wait. She'd even made Gena and Anne swear to remain silent.

And so the weekend passed . . . slow, but productive. Juniper spent most of the time working on her solo for the talent show—that and an occasional peek under her socks to make sure that article wasn't just a dream.

★ ★ ★

On Monday, Juniper saw Caitlin Greeley at her desk, in her usual position—hiding behind her mop of hair. Juniper went about English class like nothing ever happened. Every once in a while she'd think about the article, and a cluster of butterflies would flitter in her stomach. What would she feel like tonight at the meeting? *Argh!*

Things seemed to be going well until fourth period. As Juniper headed to her locker, she spotted one problem that would never go away—or make that two: the Snotty Twins. They were both standing in her way, hands on hips.

"Thought we'd just stop over and say good-bye," Beth said, curling her lip.

Juniper cocked an eyebrow at them. "You going somewhere?"

"No, but you are," Beth answered. "Mrs. Greeley has a petition so long it'd wrap around the mall."

"So," Juniper said, trying to get around them to her locker.

"So, you are going to be expelled, and it serves you right."

"Yeah," Nicole concurred.

Juniper stopped and turned. "Jeez, Nicole, I can never guess which face you're talking from. What happened to 'I'm on your side.'"

"You're full of it," Nicole said.

"'Bye now," Beth said, grinning.

Nicole marched off with her, but turned back to say, "We'll miss you at the talent show."

Juniper got her math book out and slammed the locker door. She could still hear the Snotty Twins giggling down the hall.

★ ★ ★

When Juniper stepped outside that night, the air smelled like rain. She double-checked her pocket three times to make sure the article was tucked in . . . the pendant hung safely around her neck.

Mom didn't speak, but Juniper could sense the conversation she was having inside her own brain. Mom had probably memorized an encyclopedia of facts concerning banned books and censorship. They drove to the meeting hall, leaving Jonathan and Dad sitting in front of the TV.

"Dad should've come," Mom said. "But I don't trust Jonathan alone. Not with all the problems he's been having at school."

Juniper wondered why Jonathan caught all the flack. She didn't have near the problems with name-calling that she thought she would. Maybe it was just a boy thing. When they reached the meeting, Mom slowed to a turtle's pace.

"Look at all these cars," she said. "It's packed."

Juniper felt uneasy about being the center of attention in this mob. She took in a couple of deep breaths. "I just hope some of them are on our side."

Anne's mom had saved them a couple of seats, but they soon learned that they were to sit in the front row, luckily in a different section than Mrs. Greeley. She sat across the room with her lilac Sweetums. Caitlin leaned against the wall with a crowd of other Avery students. Some were sitting cross-legged on the floor.

Up front were two long tables. The board members were already in place. She recognized a few of them, including the chairman, Mr. West, who owned the only car dealership in Avery. "Let's get these proceedings started," Mr. West said. He placed a pair of half-moon glasses on the end of his nose and shuffled some papers around. "First of all, I'd like to thank Mrs. Greeley for this turnout. We've never had such a successful attendance to a school board meeting."

Thank Mrs. Greeley? Juniper thought. *I started this mess. He should be thanking me!*

Mrs. Greeley grinned proudly.

Mr. West continued. "There seems to be an issue with a particular library book. The board has read the book in question. We've heard of the circumstances with the book report. And we've had a private meeting with Mr. Chapman and Mrs. Thompson."

"Private!" Mrs. Greeley blurted.

"Mrs. Greeley," Mr. West said. "Would you like to tell us why you are challenging this book, and issuing accusations against the young student in question?"

Mrs. Greeley rose from her chair. "It's quite obvious, isn't it? What went on in that classroom was devil worship."

The crowd broke into excited murmurs. "Quiet!" Mr. West said. "Those are strong words, Mrs. Greeley."

Mrs. Greeley dug a small black book from her purse. "If I may read a passage from the Bible."

"You may not," Mr. West interrupted. "Put it away."

"Excuse me?" Mrs. Greeley said, shock written on her face.

"This is a school proceeding. Separation of church and state. It's unconstitutional to read from a religious text."

Mrs. Greeley huffed, then produced a folder. "But this is not unconstitutional," she said. She opened it up and thumbed through some papers, all filled with signatures in two neat columns. She stomped forward and placed it in front of Mr. West.

He eyed it for a moment, then looked up. "I think I'd like to hear from Miss Lynch."

Juniper's mom shot up from her seat. "Since you brought the constitution into it— "

"Wait." Mr. West looked over his glasses at Juniper's mom. "I'd like to hear from Miss Lynch. Your daughter."

"But Mr. West—"

Juniper stood up and put her hand on Mom's arm. She knew the only way to truly communicate, to let Mom know things would be okay, was with eye contact. Mom nodded and sat down, although Juniper could read defeat in her eyes.

Mr. West smiled. "Miss Lynch—Juniper, you have caused a real ruckus in this town."

"I didn't mean to," Juniper said, her mouth as dry as the day she gave her book report.

"Could I hear your side of the story?"

"I think you've already heard it," Juniper said. "But I have something else you might like to see. I found it at the library." She dug the article out of her pocket with trembling hands. The pendant grew warm, giving her a little more confidence. She unfolded it and laid it on top of Mrs. Greeley's petition.

"Interesting," Mr. West said, nodding. He passed it to the other board members.

"What is it?" Mrs. Greeley said, hopping up and busting forward.

"Maybe you can explain this," Mr. West said.

"Yes, ma'am," Juniper agreed. "We'd all like to hear the story behind this article. How you hired a psychic to find your dog."

The crowd broke into a full tizzy. Juniper could see Anne and Gena standing in the back grinning.

"Silence!" Mr. West shouted. "Mrs. Greeley, are you familiar with the term 'the pot calling the kettle black'?"

"This was different," Mrs. Greeley said, spinning into her own tizzy. "He was a professional. He's helped the Houston Police Department."

Mr. West stood up. "In light of the new information Miss Lynch has provided, I think we've heard enough. Give us a few minutes to convene privately."

Mrs. Greeley had turned a moldy shade of green. "But Mr. West!"

There were mixed comments floating up from the crowd. Some of it was laughter. But the loudest laughter of all came from the side wall. Caitlin Greeley was chuckling it up big time.

★ ★ ★

Gena and Anne practically plowed over Juniper with excited hugs when the school board dismissed the accusations against her. Mrs. Thompson shook her hand and whispered, "That research paid off, huh?"

But Mom was just plain sappy over the whole thing. "Should I have doubted that my baby wouldn't find the perfect solution?" She smothered her with kisses, squeezing her in front of everyone who approached. "My little honor student," Mom continued. "She's a great dancer, but I'm wondering if maybe she's predestined to be a lawyer."

"Or detective," Gena said.

"I don't know," Juniper said, trying to hide her embarrassment. "I mostly used intuition on this one. Maybe I'm predestined to be a psychic."

Mom squeezed her tightly one more time, and they headed out to the car. "Dairy Treat?" Mom asked.

Juniper slumped down in the seat, exhausted. "Let's just go home."

CHAPTER 13

Cockeyed Confessions

J uniper fully expected to enter Avery Middle School with loads more pats on the back and kids saying, "Great job!" But it wasn't like that at all. She still got lots of sneers as well as smiles. The teachers seemed to be her biggest admirers, congratulating her at every opportunity.

When she entered English class she saw Caitlin Greeley looking up at her as though she'd been waiting on a board of tacks.

"Juniper, I'm so sorry I caused this problem. I really didn't mean to."

Juniper was in too good a mood to hold a grudge. "It's all right, even though you did run home and tell your mom that day."

"No, I didn't. I went out and bought the book. Mom wanted to know what I was reading and how come. I didn't think she'd go ballistic. Really."

Juniper didn't know what to say. She'd figured Caitlin all wrong from the start.

"I got into some big trouble last night," Caitlin continued.

"Why?"

"Because I laughed. Mom grounded me. But big deal. It's not like I go very many places anyway."

"I can't believe you laughed," Juniper said. "She's your mother."

Caitlin shook her head. "I wonder sometimes. She loves that squeaky little mutt more than she loves me. And before Sweetums it was Lee-lee. Mom has a thing for miniature dogs."

"I really thought you did all that on purpose," Juniper said. "I'm sorry."

Caitlin looked puzzled. "But I told you I was on your side. You read the note I gave you."

It was like the clouds had parted and Juniper could finally see the sun. "I thought that note was from Nicole."

"Nicole Hoffman? Why would she write that note? That girl is stuck up."

Juniper giggled and faced front in her seat. "And we sure don't need a petition to know how many people agree with us about that."

★　★　★

After school, Gena and Anne caught Juniper in the hall just before the talent show rehearsal. "Got your solo down?" Anne asked.

"Of course," Juniper said. She'd had all weekend to practice.

"Just make sure you don't do any E.S.P.," Gena said.

Juniper didn't get it. "I'm dancing, not reading the tarot."

Gena grinned. "E.S.P. Extra silly poses."

"I can't believe we fell for that one again," Anne said.

"I gotta go." Juniper stepped around them to head backstage. "Are you going to watch the rehearsal?" she called back.

"I've got cheer practice," Anne said.

Gena shrugged. "I'll watch. Until Carter Adams pulls out his violin. My nerves do have limits."

Juniper waited, wanting to say something, but not sure how to put it. Gena and Anne were the best friends anyone could have. They'd stuck by her—even broke up with a boyfriend because of her. She wanted to thank them, but she didn't want to sound all mushy. "Hey guys . . ."

Anne and Gena stopped and looked. Juniper smiled. "I owe you."

Anne strolled over and pulled the pendant into view. "You got that right. You owe me one yellow marble."

The girls laughed as they each went off to enjoy their afternoon.

ABOUT DOTTI ENDERLE

Dotti Enderle is a Capricorn with E.S.P.—extra silly personality. She sleeps with the Three of Cups tarot card under her pillow to help her dream up new ideas for the Fortune Tellers Club. Dotti lives in Texas with her husband, two daughters, a cat, and a pesky ghost named Shakespeare. Learn more about Dotti and her books at:

www.fortunetellersclub.com

Here's a glimpse of what's ahead in Fortune Tellers Club #8, *The Ghost of Shady Lane*

CHAPTER 11

Haunting the Past

Mr. Nicholson's statement caught Anne off guard. "Uh . . . we'd like to ask you some questions," she said.

He closed his half-moon eyes for a moment, then opened them wide. "Don't go near old Boogerman's House, or goblin bells will toll. 'Cause Boogerman's just the Devil himself, and he'll swallow you up whole."

Anne shuffled back a step and glanced nervously at Gena. Gena's mouth had turned a chalky blue-white color. She turned to Juniper and noticed her face had gone pale too. "Mr. Nicholson?" Anne said, her voice cracking.

"You've seen her, haven't you?" he said again.

"Just a picture of her."

He suddenly perked up and gave her a thin, crooked smile. "Caught her on film, huh? Now that's something I thought would never happen."

Anne glanced at Juniper and Gena again, then said, "I'd like to know what happened the night you saw her. It's for a school report. And can I record it on my tape recorder?" She reached into her backpack for it.

"Yeah," he nodded. "I'll tell you what I saw."

Anne set the recorder on the desk by him. "Start at the beginning."

"You girls might want to take a seat there."

The three of them sat on the edge of the bed. Anne never took her gaze from Mr. Nicholson.

"It was so long ago, you'd think it might eventually fade. 'Course, I always prayed it would. But I can still see her as clearly as I see you." He pointed a knobby, trembling finger at her.

Anne looked at his eyes with their half-closed lids. She wondered how clearly he really could see.

"I've been all around the world," he continued. "I've seen men in India walking on fiery coals, Haitians summoning Voodoo magic, and a man who could levitate himself five inches off the ground while standing up. But nothing compares to her . . . the Gray Lady."

Anne heard Gena suck in a shaky breath. She realized they were all a bit rattled. But this was so important to her . . . or her report, she kept telling herself.

"It was hot that summer," Mr. Nicholson said. "July. A real scorcher. I was only eleven at the time. I ran with a couple of boys named Buddy and Sal. They were a little older and only let me hang around 'cause I was their go-fer. 'Wilber, go-fer some ice cream for us.' 'Wilber, go-fer the baseball, it flew over the fence again.' Anything they asked for, I'd go for it. I really looked up to those two.

"So on that hot July night, when Sal said we should spend the night in Boogerman's house, I almost lied and told them I was sick. Nothing was going to get me inside that house. But Buddy said he'd read in the paper that there was a one hundred dollar reward for anyone who could stay there overnight—from dusk till dawn. He and Sal said we'd split the reward three ways. That money was so tempting to me, and I figured we'd be safe if there were three of us. We'd be able to look out for each other."

Anne absorbed every word. Particularly the last part. She knew his friends would betray him. How sad. She felt blessed to have two best friends who would stay beside her, even if it scared the snot out of them, like right now.

Mr. Nicholson lowered his head, then peered their way. Anne wondered if his attention span was suffering, as his daughter had said. Finally, he began again.

"About eight o'clock. That's when the sun was just setting behind that house. We slipped around and snuck in the back way. Nobody would see. Right then I wondered why we were doing that. I asked Buddy, 'Don't we need some kind of witness that we spent the night here? How are we going to prove we did it so we can collect the reward?' Buddy just snickered, then said, 'There's three of us, ain't there? We're our own witnesses.' I had no reason to doubt him.

"Now the backdoor went into the kitchen, see, and Sal jimmied the lock with a piece of copper wire. We had no problem getting in. We each had a flashlight, but Buddy was the only one to turn his on. We decided to take turns to save the batteries.

"Now I figured we'd sit up all night by the backdoor and not bother with the rest of the house. But Buddy said the rules were you only collected the reward if you stayed in the attic. I felt my stomach turn over about a dozen times. That money didn't sound so rewarding anymore. I knew I was stuck though. I couldn't let them think I was a baby. So I followed those two right up to the attic door."

Anne watched his expression change. His gaze became distant, as though his mind were reliving each moment.

"Funny thing about that door. It was small. Such a small door . . . even for a kid. I held the flashlight while Buddy and Sal pushed at it. They both had to push hard just to get it opened. I guess the wood had swollen from the heat and humidity. That July heat was the devil that year.

"As Buddy and Sal went in, Sal grabbed my arm, jerking me in with them. I shined the flashlight around the room. Just a large empty attic. The floor had been painted a steel gray color, and some of the paint was chipping. Over on the far wall was a small window, clouded with dust. I shined the light up at the ceiling. You could see clear up to the rafters. And there, near the middle, was a couple of crossbeams, and a small piece of frayed rope tied to it. It looked like someone had sawed it short with a knife. Just seeing that made me want to turn and hightail it. I started backing toward the door when I heard it slam. I ran and jiggled the knob, but it was shut tight."

Mr. Nicholson rubbed his forehead again, this time like someone with a headache. His chest expanded and deflated as he took in a giant breath. Anne could hear the air rattle inside him. He cleared his throat.

"I sat down on the floor, trying not to cry. Not only was I scared, but I felt like a danged idiot. I knew those boys had played me for a fool, and if I hadn't been so terrified I might have been humiliated. But I sat still, thinking about how I could get out. I went over to the window and tried to look out. The night was like pitch, and I couldn't see a thing. I was thinking that if I could get out that way, I could shimmy down from the roof. It was during that contemplating that I heard the noise. It was a squeaking sound that I thought was probably a mouse. But there is no such thing as a mouse that has a swaying rhythm to its squeak. I turned and shined the flashlight toward the noise."

His eyes grew twice their size, and Anne became aware that she'd been holding her breath. She let it out in a long choppy wave.

"She was there. Dangling from a noose tied to the crossbeam. Swinging slowly back and forth. Her head lobbed to the side like she was resting it on her right shoulder. Her eyes bulged, and her mouth hung opened, exposing her black tongue. I was petrified, not able to move a muscle. The only noises were the creaking of that rope and the thudding of my heart. I thought I might die of sheer terror. But the frightening part hadn't even come yet.

"My mind raced, trying to figure how to get out. I tried to open the window, but it was also swollen shut. When I turned back I flashed the light on her again. Her eyes clamped shut like I was blinding her. Then she raised her head straight up and opened them again. She stared right at me, and licked her lips with that black tongue. I hollered like a banshee, barreling for the door. I dropped the flashlight and grabbed the door handle. I pulled and screamed, managing to get it open about an inch or so, but before I could reach my fingers through to pull harder, her arm went around my neck, choking me. I jerked and wiggled, still screaming—so panicked I could have died on the spot. She brought her right hand up and scratched my face with her nails. It stung like snake venom.

"I knew I had to do something quick. I grabbed at that small opening in the door and held on for dear life. She tried to tug me back, but I wouldn't let go. The door opened just enough for a scrawny kid like me to slip through. I kicked at her, still screaming. All that squirming did some good because for a split second she let go, and I shot out of there fast as I could. And with the adrenaline pumping through me right then . . . that was the fastest I'd ever run. I made it downstairs and nearly to the front door. Just as I got there, I could see her outline in the shadows, blocking my way. I shifted quickly and headed for the window. No time to stop and open it. I kicked the glass with my shoe, breaking it into jagged shards. I jumped through, cutting my arm as I leapt. I guess luck was on my side because the iron gate was open. I ran out of there and down the street, and I didn't stop until a police car came by and made me. I collapsed on the ground."

After a few moments of silence, Anne realized he'd finished the story. "They took you to jail, right?" she prompted.

He nodded, rubbing his closed eyes with his thumb and finger.

"What happened to your friends?" Juniper asked him. Her voice sounded foreign.

"I'm not sure you could call them friends," Mr. Nicholson said. "But one policeman went and asked them to validate my story. He said they were both home in bed . . . didn't know what I was talking about. The police concluded the scratches on my face were from the broken window. They drove me home, and my father had to pay a fine for my misbehavior. He probably would have punished me good except I took to my bed and didn't move or speak for three solid days. It was another week before I could bring myself to talk about it. 'Course, no one believed me."

"I believe you," Anne said, shutting off the tape recorder. "I believe every word."

★ ★ ★